Trajectory

Teverly Swinson

BookLeaf
Publishing

Presentation by *BookLeaf Publishing*

Web: www.bookleafpub.com

E-mail: info@bookleafpub.com

ISBN: 9789358367416

First edition 2023

I dedicate this book to me. Sometimes I think those who give freely struggle to give freely to themselves. So this book is dedicated to myself with all the love and gratefulness I may wish upon others ♡

ACKNOWLEDGEMENT

I acknowledge my creator, God who created me and enables me to create. As well as my Lovely mother Dora who was always my biggest support and believer throughout my creative endeavors ♡

PREFACE

A memoir of odes from time changing to how time may change us.

I Know A Girl

I know a girl that says "GOODBYE"
Goodbye to her emotions and the way she feels
inside
"GOODBYE"
To the ones that "care"
 Because for someone to love her
 makes her feel scared
Then says "GOODBYE" to you
Because I'm just that
The girl who's pure heart has been viciously
attacked
So I say "GOODBYE" to truly being attached
Say "HELLO" to the girl with the broken heart
The heart that stopped beating when life broke it
apart

Lost

The days seem to pass you by
You sit still while life takes its daily ride
Thoughts come in and thoughts go out Wishing
one would plant itself and the answer will sprout
out
The light and the dark are irrelevant
The bark and the bite are precedent
The day and the night are waste and spent
You may even feel your heaven/hell bent
Completely numb in a sense
Lost in a world of your own repent

Here

Existence from what you witness has to be self
malicious
You will never know real wishes while painting
pictures with the fictitious
What a pitiful regime,
I get you feel you can do no better than
This is where you fade away then reemerge from
within
This is a excellent lesson and I prefer to be the
professor in when there is no end to the begin

Existence

Floating, drifting, wishing, missing,
Diminishing, lost, open and closed off
Hiding, searching and finding
Lying,crying and guiding
Exciting, mesmerizing memories and extremities
Perfection please, there is no need
When we are free to be
Floating, drifting and wishing
Missing and uplifting
Lost, open and closed off
Hiding, searching and citing
Crying, lying and guiding
Exciting, mesmerizing memories
And extremities
Perfection, please there is no need
When we are FREE to just BE…

I love you, You love me?

"I love you, you love me... we're a happy
family"
Thinking back to when I use to watch Barney..
I was probably thinking then man this is corny..
I don't really know any happy families..
And everybody don't got daddy's..
Not at least ones that's at home..
And really who hugs..
Born alone die alone..
Living like strangers in a home
You ever feel so alone?
Like what you know is not what you know
And whether to come or go
And what you feel is unknown
And that just sets the tone
For days to come of wondering
That you push to the back of your head
Think about it before bed
But you just lie awake instead
See I never wished i was dead
Just wished things were different
Like more forreal, stopped wishing
Started not to care
So When you here
You just there...

Call Waiting

Here I will stand non affected
The naysayers, yeah they feeling real rejected
See I will never bow down
Even when I must crawl
Nose high, pointed to the sky
So that I never stumble and fall
Mama taught me to always stand tall Everyone
could be on the opposite side But even still,
forget them all
And yes I believe in uplifting
But some people love the floor
They stay and glorify the bottom
As long as no one else wants more
And when you start to stand out
They try to hit you to the core
But u must build up that wall
 For the beyond pitiful
See they cant help themselves
 That's what they were built for
But I'm God made Mama made
 And I'm going to answer my call
 So have Nikki Negativity and Danni Drama
leave a voice message
 Because right now I'm on the phone with my
blessings

And yes sometimes my fingers want to get to pressing
Click over throw a fit and say forget these lessons
 But I have better things to put my best in So I can give to those who gave to me when they had less than

That Pain

You can't give a hug a smile or a laugh
To ease that pain
You can't replay a memory,have a talk take a
walk
To ease that pain
Your heart it will stain
The reminiscing, some may say it will work
But it makes things worse
And that pain still hurts
You can go through the motions
Cry and shed all the tears you holding But that
pain is still there lurking
Then you Remember that won't ease that pain
That Pain is forever and will always remain

Love Story

It was like I was cursed
Hocus pocus us interloped
Abra cadabra love comatose
First were best friend's then were enemies
 My frenemy gets the best of me
His love is forever testing me
Guilty pleasures and hateful extasy
Addicted to the worst and best of me
 I swore this was the last time
I said it was the last time, the last time
But now we're back at it
Love rewind...

Inspiration for "Love Story" by: Tevi Ann

Solace

What you find warms your heart
Does not have to be yours to share
What brings you peace is not required to be
enjoyed in a pair
Your fondest memories and darkest hours can
belong to you and you only
But if you yourself live in them your solace will
be lonely
Solace is for a moment of moments that may
never return
So enjoy the moment as if it's the only one

Caterpillar

I came to get Queen size rings and tings
Rule over beams and reams
Fly over seas and swim in oceans
Break land with my bare hands
See stars from far away lands
Feel the softest fabrics against my skin
Survive and thrive from within
Connect and break connection
Be revert and reverend
Caterpillar turned to a butterfly
 I came to make it flutter

Grace

Every day I give thanks for grace
My loyalty is not up for debate
You couldn't put up enough for me to change the stakes
My word is something they could never ever take
They need to know their place
Because I run at my pace Always protect my space
Never cared what nimrods had to say
Same imbecile just a different day
They swear they're in the game
However they never play
They just watch from the sidelines
With too much to say
But never enough to pay
Equivalent of chump change
Those minute coins could never disrupt my day
A penny for your thoughts
Or is it a heart for a heart

Inspiration for "Grace" by:Tevi Ann

Distance

Which once was a sacred routine is now a thing
of the past
Not long ago but the distance seems very vast
The Distance makes us strangers
That will never again cross paths
Who she was then
I do not know her now
I've grown from her
She's grown from me
We grew into one sound
Grew into one heartbeat
One melody and one heartbreak
One symphony and one earthquake
Unmistakable resilience that takes lifetimes to
create
Mind versus hearts debate
Thoughts and emotions that dissipate
disassociate
Understanding that takes lifetimes to
create,escape and awake
Reverence of the lives we make, take and fate
Whether it's too little or too late
Divine willing we fight another day
Another will in ourselves to take
To rejoice and remake

To destroy and curate
To be forever great
Grateful that she's not where she was today
Nourishment from a journey that taught her a
greater way

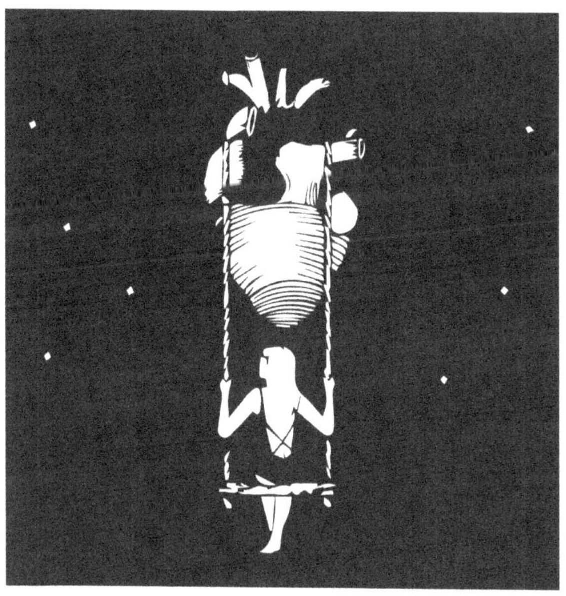

Free in 3D

Feeling free...
But what is free ?
Is it measured by certain amounts of money?
Does it grant you the wings to fly?
Does it protect you from never having to saying
goodbye ?
Never having tears fall from your eyes ..
The simplest answer is no
Because you will always pay as you go You pay
with your time
You pay with your mind
you will pay with your heart
you will pay as soon as your very first breath
starts
You will pay how you weigh
You will pay to play everyday
And I know it sounds cliche
But life is truly what you make it
How you mold and create it
How you...DO YOU!

Your Highness

New Queen on the scene
I came to over throw
You could never catch up with me
Your stuck with me
No invites
Only RSVP
Come up with
Disrupt me
I let you know
Just happen to be doing it confidentially
So the vibe is subsequently
The presence of me makes it evidently
It's easy to see
Quite rudimentary
Quite contrary
To one's beliefs
They think im affiliated
When I'm the one that orchestrated
I can never be duplicated
Because I am thee Originator
They try and compete
But they can't get in my arena nor get a ticket for
a seat
You have war with me or nothing
Isn't that something

Inspiration for "O.T.G." by: Tevi Ann

Escape

Can't penetrate this gate
Your asking for death as your fate
You asking for forgiveness
Your too late
They keep making lefts
Thinking they know what's right
We met up at a round about
But I left them at the light
I Hit the gas and I was out of sight
Had my brakes on ice
Speeding to my new life
Hatred out of spite
They can't get this fly
Like a misle
 I surpass the sky
Dancing on the planets
I saw it with my own third eye
You can add three and two everyday
You still won't get five
I have the whole supply
You can't divide this pie
I have the whole supply
And then some
Coated with fire
Butterflies and brimstone

I have the four
the three
the two
And the one

Inspiration for "Pop" by Tevi Ann

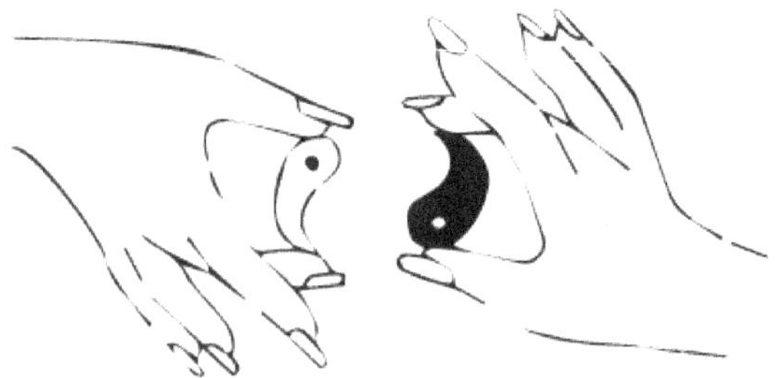

Leaving

He was calling and calling
She was stalling and stalling
She didn't want to tell him that her heart had
fallen
For another mister
She felt his heart was bigger
His attitude wasn't sour and he wasn't always
bitter
She no longer wanted to be his lady
Nor wanted him as her mister

Shining

The sun's shining
I'm shining
 So it's perfect timing
I previously made some bad plays
But currently off to enjoy better days
One for every week I've been gave
They've tried to to flip the scale
However I have already prevailed
I am never stopping to no avail
Equipped from above
Embraced by the love

Inspiration for "Shinola" By:Tevi Ann

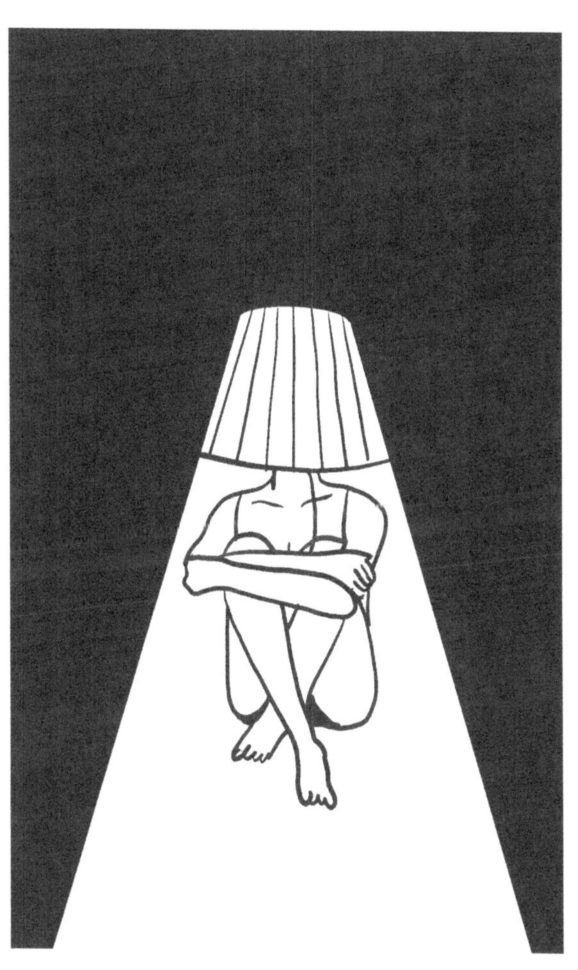

Chapters

One ends
One begins
One may include many things
One may include nothing at all
One may be full of triumphs
One may be full of many flaws
One may be filled with great love
One may be filled with great loss
One may be filled with lessons
One may be filled with being lost
One may be filled with connection
One may be filled with hope
No matter what they may be filled with
It may or may not comfort you to know
One ends
One begins